IT WAS THROUGH HER LIPS SHE SPOKE...

VOLUME II

Christina-Mary Seabrook

Editing by *KarolynEditsBooks.com*

Contact author at: *christinamaryseabrook@gmail.com*

Contents

"Forever Type"

Armani, Kristian, Khloé, and Karmen

PART ONE

Many Lives, Same Pain (Many Sufferings)

Hell on Earth

I've been here for some time now and it hasn't become easy.
More death than births.
This world is starting to lose its meaning,
yet I feel like I've seen worse.
Remembering when I could go outside and just play
with no cares in the world,
but now it feels like hell on Earth.

Every day looking at the news that brings me no good news.
No graduation celebrations, no cure for cancer,
no black child with a high IQ.
Just painting pictures of money, madness, and mayhem,
Only to have this world look at me and mines not so perfect.

Can you remember when being a kid was just that,
being a kid?
Wearing bobos and matching clothes.
Now our kids have grown.
Not wanting nothing but social media likes
and taking others' lives.
Hell on Earth is surely where I lay my head,
not knowing if a bullet will be the thing that destroys me.
Depending on which position I play,
I can choose to hold the gun or be in front of it.
See this is the way we play
when really, I'm trying to make a way out of no way.

Sometimes I wonder if heaven is too far of a reach for me.
So, as I sit here watching the days go by,
I remember that soon I will be with my maker,
where I'll be gratefully free.

Why Didn't You Listen?

Look what we have here.
You thought you knew everything but knew nothing.
I was trying to save you
from the hardship you would have to face
but instead, you wanted to take the so-called easy way.
Now look at you looking at me
the same way I looked at my mother.
All because I thought I knew everything.

I'm not going to say I told you so,
because it won't serve a purpose.
I just hoped that you would learn from it.
I thought I was so grown and knew it all.
But in actuality, I set myself up for failure,
not thinking about the end result.
I kept repeating the history that came before you.
I thought the cycle would end with you,
but not to my surprise, you continued it.

I know a lot played a part in this
and honestly, I feel like I'm the one to blame in this.
While I thought I was giving you the tools you needed,
you found tools in places where you didn't need to travel.
Now I'm sitting here trying to understand
why you didn't listen to me, as I kiss your cold face.
Damn...

How Can You Play God?

So, I guess you immortal now?
You believe that you can cast judgement on others
or punish who you want?
You think that because you hold that gun
you control how things end for me?
You believe that you are getting justice
for the ones who thought they were immortal before you?
Do you really find that fair?

I'm just wondering what the logic is
behind playing someone you can never be.
You see, I believe that you are plagued with a hateful disease.
This disease takes over your whole body
and has you spraying through the bodies
of both the innocent and non-innocent.
Makes you believe that you're honorable or even heaven-sent.
But the truth is you're a mess.
You have past hurt that you have yet to deal with
and you cast your burdens on us with that gun in your hand.

How can you play God?
when you actually playing the devil?
You let him control your every move,
but you thinking you got all the sense in the world.
Funny how you thought you were immortal.
Now looking at you lying here with blood flowing from your body.
Now you realize you are mortal.
Here no more.

Blood-Soaked

I ran two blocks trying to get to you
and really needed you to heal me.
As I lay there, blood-soaked,
I can hear everybody calling my name
and recording, saying, "That's Junior,"
while I sit there bleeding out.

Let me rewind back a few for you.
See, I asked my mother, "Can I walk to the bodega?"
and gave her a kiss and went on my way.
Not knowing the danger, I looked ahead.
I took my journey.
Then all of sudden, I was running for my life.
I was scared, confused, and thought,
What did I do to make them chase me?

As I entered the bodega,
I jumped over the counter trying to hide.
Too late—they found me,
and now as they drag me away, all I feel is sharp pain.
Sadly, the sharp pains were from the machetes they used
to chop and stab me up, wanting to take my life away.
As I finally break free, I run back in the bodega,
and then I run off to make it to you.

Now back to me lying across the street from you.
I just wanted to grow up and continue to make my momma proud.
I never hurt nobody.
I truly was a good kid and now I'm laying here blood-soaked
all because of mistaken identity.
All because of the decision of man.

They didn't have the right to take my just-beginning life.
So, as I lay here across from you blood-soaked,
I thought you would be my savior,
but in the end, I couldn't reach you.

Who Would Speak for Me?

I was an upcoming chef, you see.
Turned my life around and made a better me.
Was just coming from getting a bite to eat,
and a round hit me.
Who would've known it would land my face on TV.
But the question is, who would speak for me?

Just chilling with my friends
and making memories that I couldn't imagine would end.
Until that fateful night I lost my sight
and the flames engulfed me.
Look at me—I'm on TV, clear as can be.
But the question is, who would speak for me?

On my way home from getting my nephew a bite to eat,
A bullet took my life... Oh why me?
I had dreams of going to college, you see.
Now I'm trapped in my family's memory.
Hey, it's me on TV, but the question is,
who would speak for me?

Where I'm from, ain't no justice.
They would rather be silent and watch while my killer walks free.
But why should that be?
I mean the sad thing is that this is my reality.
Just remember when you see me on TV,
understand that I didn't plan to be just a memory.
I didn't plan to cause so much pain.
I wasn't finished but my purpose was done.
Yet I didn't know who would speak for me.
When will my battle be won?

I Just Wanted to See the Fireworks

My momma always told me I was going to be a star,
that I would go real far.
I could've grown to make it to the NFL,
be a person my community needed.
My momma loved the community,
and became a voice of reason within my community.
She was the epitome of calmness.
She and her coworkers were really out here
making a difference.
She was the reason I was a piece of her,
a piece now gone.

Just being a kid for the Fourth of July,
watching the fireworks go up in the sky, so bright and colorful.
Oh, what a sight to see!
Knowing what I know sometimes,
as the fireworks burst into the air.
The bullets do the same,
and now all I feel is pain.
I black out to wake up looking at my mother crying
and my body lying there.
I try to wipe away her tears, but they just continue to flow.
I just wanted to see the fireworks.
Now I sit with the Most High,
watching the beautiful fireworks in the sky.

Public Enemy Number One

They look at me like I'm a public enemy.
Truth is, I am a woman—a black woman.
Let my break it down for you.
My brothers and sister go missing
and come back with their organs missing.
Yet y'all say I'm tripping.

You paint me as a menace to your society,
when it was you who brought me here.
I left my freedom to be so-called free,
yet you still say I'm tripping.
Crazy how I'm painted as public enemy number one
when the true enemy is your people.
You take your Bible and turn it around on me,
when it is I who should be who I want to be.

You aren't a reflection of me.
You are the enemy who tries to defeat me.
You paint me as public enemy number one.
The truth is, I am a woman, a black woman.
You take my brothers and sisters
and return them with their organs missing,
yet you say I'm tripping.

PART TWO

Sis Look Up! Your Crown Is Falling

Did You Understand Your Worth?

As I sit listening to her pour her heart out,
I began to fade out.
She was the definition of beautiful.
The way she carried herself,
the way words would flow from her mouth,
to the tears she cried.
She would make time for him, him, and him.
She wanted love but not just any love.
The highest love, agape love.
Instead, she became lustful for what the world could give her,
at least what she *thought* it could.

Fading back in, I asked, "Do you understand your worth?"
She looked confused,
trying to understand what I had said.
I asked again.
Growing up, we saw the ladies in our lives
juggle male after male.
We became accustomed to trying to follow in their footsteps.
These were the women who guided us.
At least this is what we thought.
Tried to mimic their ways,
but it really didn't work out that way.

More damage was just added to the pain.
Looking for the pieces within him, him, and him.
Trying to put out the flame,
that was deadly and staking it's claim.
Will she ever be the same?
"What is worth?" she asked.

And I replied,
"The dictionary defines worth as 'the value equivalent to that of someone or something under consideration or the level at which someone or something deserves to be valued or rated.'
When you see yourself as more than a good time
and understand your full worth is valuable,
you will then understand your full potential.
Until then, you will just be the time and seconds
spent with him, him, and him.
Making your worth detrimental.
With every him, him, and him,
your worth starts to deteriorate.
Do you understand why?"

While she was still sitting with that blind look on her face,
I explained.
You haven't found that male who increases your value
and explores your hopes and dreams.
One who understands what it means
to be in the presence of a queen.
Instead, he will just decide to take your worth for his need.

Missing Something

For a while I've been half-full.
I don't smile the way I used to.
I don't shine and I've become used to it.
At times I can't articulate how I feel,
and to be honest, I haven't really been healed.

Stresses of this world have been getting to me.
I've let man play a damn trick on me.
Feels like every time I fail,
trying to understand everybody's joy and pain.
Now I sit here missing something,
and I'm trying to figure out what could it be
that causes all this pain.

What I looked for can't be found in a human.
It can't be found in money.
It can't be found in this society.
So, I look up to he who sits high.
See, he has all the answers I need.
But then he says to me,
"My child, the answers you seek
are already embedded inside of you.
I have already given you the tools
that can unlock all you seek.
You just have to believe."

The Conversation

Who are you?
What have you been through?
Can you come here?
I'm trying to have a conversation with you.
You sit here mad at the world,
because you lack understanding.
You think nobody cares about you
or all the things you've been through.
It will only take a minute.
Please let me hear it.

Oh I lack understanding, huh?
I'm so mad at the world? Go figure...
You just don't understand it.
This world wasn't in my plan.
You may think I'm so broken,
but in reality, my God had already spoken.
He said, "My child, it's time for you to go to a place.
A place where you will feel joy and pain.
It may get rough but in time,
you will understand that I am with you and in you."

My God already knew what I would go through,
but it was up to me to choose.
You see, I've become used.
I'm like a pretty pendant that has tarnished,
looking to shine again.

So may I ask, What did you choose?
And did it consume you?
Because it wasn't *what* I chose

but *who* I chose.
He was a good friend of my God,
at least that's what I thought.
Lucifer was his name.
I had chosen pain.
Not knowing Lucifer had heard when my God spoke to me.
It was all in Lucifer's plan as he'd proclaimed.

I became in love with someone so deadly,
not realizing I'd started to see less of God and more of him.
Until one day, I got on my knees,
asking my God, "Please forgive me.
I seemed to have lost my way and I need you."

My God said, "My child,
do you realize I've been waiting for you?
I knew the route you would take before you chose.
My child, I never left you but instead I remain.
I had always been there; you were just in a daze.
You see Lucifer fed off your pain, and as he proclaimed.
It was your prayer to me that restored your broken frame.
As I end this conversation,
remember I will always be there.
My child, you have finally realized
that I am in you and with you.
Now smile again my child,
because you finally realized I was all you needed."

Your Beautiful Death

Why are we here again?
You told me not to fear again
but yet again, you brought me back to the pain.
I thought we had healed you before,
but now you just going down memory lane.
I thought we restored your soul,
but I guess time doesn't heal all wounds.

Yes, my melanin bruised, but I am restored again.
But I have to lay something to rest.
My life hasn't all been a mess,
but some of the stuff I've been through,
I put *myself* through.
My actions were equal to either happiness or heartbreak.
Today I give myself the power to say, "I forgive me."

I forgive me for bringing certain deaths upon me,
and I don't mean physically.
Mentally, I've allowed males in my life
and turned it around drastically.
From the domestic violence to the verbal abuse.
I let them use me up and leave me empty.
Now it's time for me to let the memories die.
This beautiful death is the start of a new beginning.
I've forgiven myself for my own actions
and now I am completely free.

Rebalancing Myself

I'm sitting here really trying to understand
how I ended up here.
I've given you my mind, body, and soul,
yet you didn't see the beauty in them.
Instead, you unbalanced me.
I've been wobbly ever since.
You used to complete me,
but now you have just used me up.

You've made me feel less than.
Even when I try to stand, you bring me down.
I want to forgive you but every time I try,
you give me one more reason to hate you.
I start to think I've healed myself from you,
but sadly, here you come again.
Telling me all the things I thought of you and me.
Sadly, my memories of your hurting replay in my mind.

In order for me to rebalance myself,
I have to first forgive me.
See, I let you use me and hurt me.
I continued to see the good in you and ultimately,
I was the one to blame.
You see, I gave too much of me.
So, as I focus more on me,
I have gotten rid of you and poured more into me.
I am rebalancing me.

PART THREE

What's Your Pleasure?

In This Room

As I wait for you to come in this room,
I began to remember how it felt the last time we met.
The way your lips explored my body,
and the way mine explored yours.
I mean, baby, the way you ate it like it was the last supper,
I could tell that you wanted to please me but also feed me.
But we ain't through.
The longer I don't see you, the more I want you.
Like Jodeci, I fiend for you.

This room was our sanctuary,
and I was looking for a healing.
I mean, I was looking for you to cleanse me oh so deeply.
So, while I sit waiting for you to come into this room,
I already know what we gonna do.
Shit, déjà vu...
See, I'm a sinner baby and I'm probably gonna sin again,
but it's your cleansing that washes away my sin.
See, as that music plays,
and you gently caress every inch of my body,
I know it is time for us to lay.
I mean from the kisses to the booty rubs. I'm in a deep daze.
Before you, nobody ever treated me this way.
It was always them getting theirs
while I was getting played.

In this room, you licking and slurping me
while I gently lay my hands on your head.
I'm trying to control these waves,
but your tongue got the best of me, baby.
Got my legs shaking and shit.

What's that Jacquees song?
Oh yeah, I can "Feel it."
See, I give you all of me, knowing you have control of me.
We just intertwined and will always be.
Yeah, this room is our sanctuary,
and I'm a sinner baby, so come and restore my energy.

Suck Me

I'm going to get right to it.
I have no time to waste.
You know time is of the essence,
so come now and take your place.
I'm not going to lie,
I've been waiting for this great high.
Trying to decide how imma get this right.

I love it when he is deep inside me
caressing with every inch of dick and tongue inside me.
I know how it's got to be and honestly,
I love when he sucks me,
the way he slurps me up and make my legs shake.
Knowing this can't wait,
he says, "Now love, take your place."

So, as he stands up, I get on my knees.
Taking my place where he needs me.
Submitting to his command.
I lick my lips and give it a kiss.
He knows what's about to go down.
I began to take every inch of him as our eyes connect.
When he fucks my face and rolls his eyes back,
I know he's mine.
Feeling his dick throbbing
and the warmth of his cum drowning me,
he whispers, "Damn, I love it when you suck me..."

Fantasy

As he kissed on my lips, I knew this was it.
I couldn't hide it.
Like Medusa, I looked into his eyes, and he was hypnotized.
But to my surprise,
he was what I needed between my thighs.
Gently touching my hips,
I could imagine how my shit would grip his dick.

I mean, the way I would suck on his lips
and proceed to suck on his dick.
Whewww I could just imagine it.
The way I would ride his dick ,
and he would come quick,
but I would love every moment of it.
The way his moans would drive me crazy,
and I would cum baby.
Listen please, don't think I'm being shady
because baby, you'll drive me crazy.
But I could never be his baby.

The way he kiss my inner thighs would just drive me wild.
I mean, can you imagine the things he would do to me?
The way he would handcuff me to the bed
and have his way with me.
As crazy as it sounds, I was always down.
Tempting, right?
But for now, he's out of mind and out of sight.
You see, all the things he was doing to me wasn't reality.
It just was my fantasy...

With Every Stroke

It had begun,
from the kisses to licking and sucking.
He devoured me completely,
taking me to a higher level with every stroke.
When he pulled it out, ate it, and put that dick back in...
Shit, I damn near fainted.

With every stroke, he was taking the breath from me
but also filling me up just the same.
It started with the words, "I miss you"
and I replied, "I missed you too," as he inserted.
As we slipped and slid,
we realized it was showtime.
So I began to arch my back and let him attack.
With every stroke, we became more and more as one.
I started to fiend him, knowing he's the one.

With every stroke, I became hypnotized.
I mean, in a deep trance.
Trying to figure out how he took my soul,
and would this last?
With every stroke, he came more and more...
deeper and deeper...
I began to speak; at least that's what I think.

I became entangled in his web.
No lies, but with pride I enjoyed the ride.
With every stroke, I could feel his kinetic energy.
I felt like his body transferred to mines, and mines to his.
He began to give me his all.

And as I woke in a cold sweat,
I realized with every stroke, he was my reality.
But for now, he would stay where I wanted him,
which was in my fantasy.

Play Wit It

Alright it's time for me to unwind.
I had a long day and I need to fade away.
Let me put on something sexy,
or maybe I should just get straight to it?
See, I've been needing it all day and imma release it.

I tried waiting for him to come,
but I'm a little impatient today.
Listen, I told you I just want to fade away.
I'm already horny baby and I can't let that go to waste.
I got to do what I got to do.
Imma take control of this situation, you see.
It's only temporary, but I'll manage.
So, let's begin...

As I suck on them
I can feel how wet he makes me feel.
He knows what I want and how I like it.
So, as he rubs on my clitoris,
I began to feel this blissful ecstasy.
He's tasting me and I'm tasting me.
Never knew how real this could be.
He's just taking over me.
He says, "How you want it, fast or slow?"
and at this point, I'm just trying not to blow.
With a steady pace, I'm just trying to stay on top.
We competitive, so we try to see who will cum off top.

Switching positions,
I know we about to be here for a couple of hours.
I mean, the way he going deep,

I'm trying not to moan but I can't control it.
He got me in my zone,
and damn it, I love when he's in control.
Touching my soul,
he finds what another hadn't all these years.
He's touching my g-spot, kissing me,
and smacking my ass all at the same time .

I said I wanted to fade away.
So, as I finish squirting, I open my eyes
and remember that I was impatient today.
So I decided to just play wit it...

Nectar Oh So Sweet

As she walked into the door,
I knew she was what I wanted to explore.
She looked so innocent, but the way she looked at me,
I could tell she wanted her more.
You see, pussy was what she adored but dick gave her more.
As I sat watching her undress,
I could picture the rest.

As she lay her body down,
I could hear the sounds of my girl licking down.
I became so aroused.
Slurping that sweet nectar we had found.
With every lick, she began to drown.
It was my duty to make them smile.
See, she was the appetizer, and I was their main course.
So, as I began to drill, I began to feel her warmth.
The fucked-up thing was that I couldn't forget it.
I mean—she was *with it.*

As she walked in the door,
she already knew what she had come for.
You see, she would give it to me oh so easily.
So easily that she would beg for more.
She knew I had a man, but he was just part of the plan.
The way I lay her down, I remember the sound.
The nectar oh so sweet,
I began to drown.
You see, she was my appetizer,
and he was our main course meal.
As he drilled, I could feel the thrill.

I knew what I came here for.
She was what I adored.
So, as she began to eat my nectar oh so sweet,
she took the life out of me.
I was her appetizer, and he was our main course meal.
As he drilled, she could feel the thrill,
but I knew what was real.

It was part of the plan.
We began to hear him make those sounds.
The way our lips went down,
he was amazed and in a daze.
As we go round for round,
we can't give up now.
So, as I rode his face,
she already knew her place.
Our nectar oh so sweet.
The threesome complete.

Blissful Ecstasy

I don't know what has come over me.
I've become oh so damn horny.
My legs began to get weak because she needs me.
She likes the way I treat her and beat her,
the way we become so high in ecstasy.
Can you feel it? I mean really feel it?
Blissful ecstasy so sweet.

Now put on a show for me, baby.
I like when you get nasty with me.
Show me you in control,
because this blissful feeling is where I need to be.

Alone in the room,
she puts on a show I just can't ignore it.
The way she rides it, she's in control.
As she places her hands on my chest, she begins to ride it.
Starting on her toes and then on her knees.
With the ride, she takes every breath from me.

PART FOUR

What's Your Story?

Could You Handle It?

So you want to know the real me?
As if what you see isn't what you get.
You'd rather me tell some shit that's irrelevant
just to make you feel like we've connected.
Have you second guessing,
trying to learn these lessons
while trying to be a blessing.

But since you insist, let me break it down for you.
I was born into this world with all the odds stack against me,
but I began to receive my two blessings.
They set the foundation of the man I would grow up to be.
Now comes me falling for somebody
of whom I believed we would forever be.
But instead, who gave me a little me, so I'm grateful.
I have had my share of ups and downs,
but I got up and turned that shit around.

You might think that what I'm telling you
is something I'll tell the next,
but understand what I'm giving you is truth.
I'm giving you the raw me,
my flaws and all me.
Never been ashamed of it.
I just felt others weren't worth it.
I wonder, would you complete my story?
Could you heal what's been broken?
Have our energies been interchanged?
So, I simply ask this: Could you handle it?

Young King

I know that the males you've watched growing up
ain't been showing you the right way.
Instead, they showing how to die.
I ain't going to act like this world has made it easy for you,
young king
but I can't stand to see you left here in fear
and wondering if this is God's will.

Young king, do you understand that your potential
is what they truly fear?
The potential to be a doctor, lawyer, judge, and so many other things.
They fear what they don't understand,
but young king, hold your head up high.
You were meant to be a leader not a follower,
so I won't accept anything less.
Young king, you are simply the best.

One day you will be running our world.
One day you'll have a family.
You may even have a young king yourself.
Just remember, young king, be all that you can be,
and don't let where you lay your head
be the place where you lay dead.
Bring life to this world because, young king, you deserve it.
Be a true king.

Public Enemy Number One

They look at me like I'm a public enemy.
Truth is I'm a woman. But also, a black woman.
Let me break it down for you.
My brothers and sisters go missing,
and come back and they organs missing.
Yet y'all say I'm tripping.

You paint me as a menace to your so-called society,
when it was you who brought me here.
I left my freedom to be so-called free.
Yet y'all say I'm tripping.
Crazy how I'm painted as public enemy number one,
when the true enemy is your people.
You take your Bible and turn it around on me,
when it is I who should be who I want to be.

You aren't a reflection of me.
You are the enemy who tries to defeat me.
You paint me as public enemy number one.
The truth is, I am woman. A black woman.
You take my brothers and sisters
and return them with their organs missing,
but yet you say I'm tripping.

Living with Regrets

Damn, here we are back here again.
Trying to figure out
how I could've changed how our story ends.
I mean, I thought we had more time to build our story,
but look what life has done to you.
I always thought the world of you.
You see, I knew you were going to be something special.
I just couldn't put my finger on what it would be.

I remember us just growing up and being truly ourselves.
See, everybody thought they knew me,
but you knew the true me.
You knew my heartbreaks, my mistakes,
my breakdowns, and my uplifts.
Until the day we decided to go our separate ways.
You wanted the life of luxury,
and I wanted to get it the way I saw fit.

No falling out, just two people making adult decisions.
I wish I could've told you
that you were more than them streets you called home.
But I understand it.
No mom, no dad, and the streets were all you've ever known.
Now I fast forward to the last day I ever laid eyes on you.
Regrets of me not telling you to get out them streets.
Now you lay six feet deep.

Live My Truth

I've always expected you to accept me.
You gave birth to me but now you neglect me.
Not understanding I created me.
Momma, you taught me to love myself, be me, and live carefree.
But lately, you haven't been practicing what you preach.

You say you love me,
but because I choose to love who genuinely loves me,
you disregard me.
You tell me, "The daughter I know has lost her soul,
and I will not watch you do it."
So, I must go.
I've known people who agree to disagree,
but all in all, still genuinely love and try to be there for me.

But yet momma, I long for you to accept me.
I long for you to truly love me.
I don't want you to wait until life goes by and then you realize.
So, I'm going to say it now,
"I forgive you and still think the world of you."
I just have to live in my truth.
My truth allows me to be free.
It allows me to be unapologetically me.

God Sent Me to You

Before I was sent down to you,
God had already brought life to me.
You see, he'd already decided who I would be.
He told me that life is me.
Down on Earth is where I grew
while sitting inside of you.
I could hear everything that you went through.
I remember the day that you were going to give me death,
but God sent an angel down
to help you change my path.

As the months grew longer,
I was starting to get too big to stay inside of you.
Now it's time to enter into this world
to see who my creator gave me to.
Wow! she's beautiful, and to my surprise,
she loved every moment of me.
As she smiled, I yelled with joy.
She gave me a name that God had already told me,
but something about the way she said it was mesmerizing.
She didn't know the journey bestowed on her,
but she was ready for it.

I knew an older brother and two sisters would come after me,
and we would be the epitome of our mother's roots.
But as I got older, I realized
that I had to create the person I wanted to be.
That road became shaky.
I was teased and bullied because of how God created me.
I began to dibble and dabble in a few things
and let the sin of this world take place.

Now I'm back to where I started from.
God said, "I sent you to this place
because I knew you would be able to handle everything,
good or bad.
Now child, rest; your journey has just begun."

Made in the USA
Middletown, DE
02 October 2021

48690892R00038